D1084399

Lions

and Other Wild Cats

Concept and Product Development: Editorial Options, Inc.
Series Designer: Karen Donica
Book Author: Steven A. Horak

For information on other World Book
products, visit us at our Web site at
http://www.worldbook.com

For information on sales to schools and libraries
in the United States, call 1-800-975-3250.

For information on sales to schools and libraries
in Canada, call 1-800-837-5365.

World Book, Inc.
233 N. Michigan Avenue
Chicago, IL 60601

Library of Congress Cataloging-in-Publication Data

Horak, Steven A.
    Lions and other wild cats / [Steven A. Horak].
      p. cm. -- (World Book's animals of the world)
    Summary: Presents information on the physical characteristics, behavior, and natural
    environment of lions and other wild cats.
    ISBN 0-7166-1226-7 -- ISBN 0-7166-1223-2 (set)
    1. Lions--Juvenile literature. 2. Felidae--Juvenile literature. [1. Lions. 2. Cat family
    (Mammals)] I. World Book, Inc. II. Title. III. Series.

QL737.C23 H67 2002
599.75--dc21   2001046708

Printed in Malaysia

1 2 3 4 5 6 7 8 9 06 05 04 03 02

Picture Acknowledgments: Cover: © Kate McDonald, Bruce Coleman Inc.; © Erwin & Peggy Bauer, Bruce Coleman Inc.;
© D. Robert Franz, Bruce Coleman Inc.; © Jeff Lepore, Photo Researchers; © Laura Riley, Bruce Coleman Inc.

© Erwin & Peggy Bauer, Bruce Coleman Inc. 17, 39; © Tom Brakefield, Bruce Coleman Inc. 4, 23, 35, 45, 55; © Tim Davis,
Photo Researchers 31; © D. Robert Franz, Bruce Coleman Inc. 33, 43; © Hamman/Heldring, Animals Animals 27; © Mike Hill,
Bruce Coleman Collection 13; © Iwago Mitsuaki, Minden Pictures 5, 59; © Stephen J. Krasemann, Photo Researchers 51;
© Pat Lanza, Bruce Coleman Inc. 15; © Jeff Lepore, Photo Researchers 49; © Sven-Olof Lindblad, Photo Researchers 25;
© Kate McDonald, Bruce Coleman Inc. 3, 19; © Joe McDonald, Animals Animals 29; © Laura Riley, Bruce Coleman Inc. 61;
© Francois Savigny, Animals Animals 21; © John Shaw, Bruce Coleman Inc. 47; © Charles G. Summers Jr., Bruce Coleman Inc.
7; © Paul Van Gaalen, Bruce Coleman Collection 5, 41; © Stan Wayman, Photo Researchers 37; © Terry Whittaker, Photo
Researchers 53, 57.

Illustrations: WORLD BOOK illustration by Michael DiGiorgio 11, WORLD BOOK illustration by Kersti Mack 9, 62.

Lions
and Other Wild Cats

Do you want to hear me roar?

World Book, Inc.
A Scott Fetzer Company
Chicago

Contents

How do my stripes help me hunt?

Where can you spot me?

Who do I look like?

What Is a Wild Cat?

Like a pet cat, a wild cat is a mammal that belongs to the cat family. Members of the cat family are also known as felines. This term comes from the word scientists use for the family of cats: Felidae *(FEE luh DEE)*.

Unlike a pet cat that is usually tame and kept in a home or yard, a wild cat lives in the wilderness and must fend for itself. Lions are wild cats. So are tigers and cheetahs. Leopards, caracals *(KAHR uh kalz),* and jaguars *(JAG wahrz)* are wild cats, too.

Wild cats and other mammals are warm-blooded, and they have body hair. Also, mammal babies drink the milk of their mothers. But unlike other mammals, most cats have retractable claws. That means that their claws can be pulled back into their paws.

Members of the cat family are carnivores *(KAHR nuh vawrz),* or meat-eaters. Four of each wild cat's teeth are long and sharp. These teeth are called canines. Wild cats use their canines to stab and to hold onto prey.

Female lion

Where in the World Do Wild Cats Live?

Wild cats live in many parts of the world. They live as far south as the tip of South America and as far north as Siberia in Asia. Australia and Antarctica are the only continents on which wild cats are not found.

Wild cats live in a wide variety of habitats. Some wild cats, such as cheetahs, prowl dry, open plains. Others, such as leopards, can be found in wet forests and swamps. Some wild cats roam on mountains and in valleys.

Lions live on only two continents—Africa and Asia. These wild cats make their homes on grassy plains or areas with both trees and grass. They aren't found in thick forests. Most lions live in hot, dry climates where the temperature can really soar. To beat the heat, lions spend much of the day resting in the brush, or an area with shrubs, bushes, and small trees.

World Map

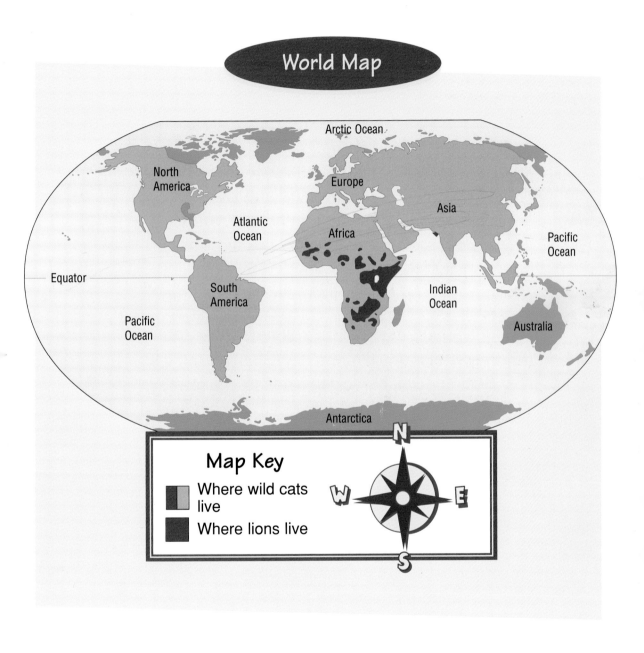

Arctic Ocean

North America

Europe

Asia

Atlantic Ocean

Africa

Pacific Ocean

Equator

South America

Indian Ocean

Pacific Ocean

Australia

Antarctica

Map Key

Where wild cats live

Where lions live

N
W   E
S

How Are a Lion and a Pet Cat Alike?

A lion and a pet cat have a lot in common. As you can see from the diagram, both have similar shapes. They have lean bodies and long tails. Both have long, pointed canines and sharp, retractable claws. Both species use their claws to climb, to hold, to fight, and to kill. And both a lion and a pet cat walk on their toes—not on the soles of their feet.

Lions spend much of their time on the ground. But they are good climbers, too—just as pet cats are. Both species can climb trees to chase prey. Also, both lions and pet cats use body language and scents to communicate. They also use calls. Lions roar. Pet cats meow. And just like pet cats, lions take catnaps!

But, in spite of all these similarities, there is one big difference. A lion is about 30 times larger than the average pet cat. Imagine having a cat that big around the house!

Diagrams of a Lion and a Pet Cat

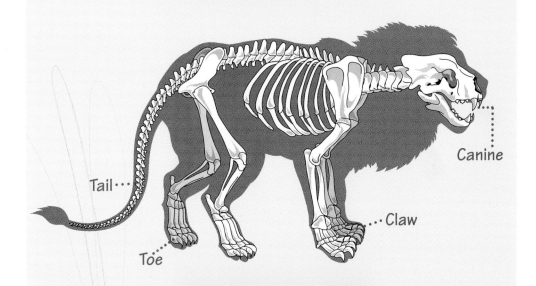

Canine

Tail

Claw

Toe

Lion skeleton

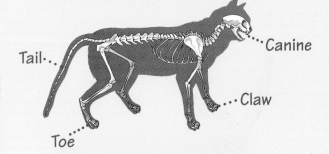

Canine

Tail

Claw

Toe

Pet cat skeleton

What Makes Lions "Kings"?

Lions are often called kings of the animal world, and it is easy to see why. Lions are among the largest of the wild cats. Most male lions weigh from 350 to 400 pounds (160 to 180 kilograms), but some weigh up to 560 pounds (250 kilograms). Including their tails, full-grown male lions are usually about 9 feet (2.7 meters) in length. They stand an average of 4 feet tall (1.2 meters) at the shoulder. Lionesses, or female lions, are slightly smaller.

But their huge size does not slow these animals down. While chasing prey, lions can reach speeds up to 35 miles (56 kilometers) per hour. That's faster than many birds can fly!

A male lion has one of the largest heads of all the wild cats. Around his head and neck is a mane of thick, long hair. This mane gives the male lion a kingly look. He is the only wild cat with a mane.

Male lion

Is a Lion's Mane Just for Show?

A mane makes an adult male lion look bigger than he really is. It is made up of long, thick fur. It may be yellow, brown, or black in color. But while a mane is striking, it's more than just for show.

The bigger mane a male lion has, the more impressive he looks to other males. And the more impressive he looks, the more likely he will become one of the leaders of a group of lions.

A majestic mane also helps a male avoid fights with other males. This is because males with less impressive manes are not likely to fight lions with longer manes. But if a male lion does get into a fight, the thick mane comes in handy. It protects a male lion's neck.

14

Male lion with
bushy mane

What Is a Pride?

Most wild cats spend nearly their whole lives on their own—but not lions. Lions spend most of their lives in groups called *prides*. A pride may include as many as seven adult males and many more females and cubs—up to 40 lions in all.

The lionesses, or female lions, of a pride are usually related to each other. And they generally stay with a pride their entire lives. Males do not stay their entire lives. But they may remain for several years. In time, they leave to join a new pride, or other males drive them off. Young males that leave a pride may spend a few years wandering together until they are strong enough to lead their own pride.

A pride's territory usually covers around 80 square miles (210 square kilometers). A pride chooses its territory based on the availability of two things: prey and water. Lions mark their territory by urinating on trees and shrubs around its border. The scent of these markings tells other lions to keep out.

Pride of lions

Why Do Lions Roar?

Lions roar to announce their territory to other lions. These calls warn other lions to stay away. Lions can roar so loudly that they can be heard up to 5 miles (8 kilometers) away. Any animal that hears the roar knows that lions are nearby. And that's usually enough to send an animal running in the opposite direction!

Lions do most of their roaring at the beginning and ending of their day. They also often roar after hunting. Sometimes, one pride will hear the roars of another pride. Lions in the first pride will answer with roars of their own.

Male lion roaring

Who Does What in a Pride?

What a lion does depends mostly on whether it is a male or a female. The adult males are responsible for defending the pride's territory against intruders. If the male lions are to remain the leaders of the pride, they must be able to drive off other groups of males that try to take over. Large males will often drive away hyenas, jackals, or other animals that wander into their territory, too.

While male lions defend the territory, females do most of the hunting. In order for a pride to survive, its lionesses must be skilled hunters. But both males and females guard any leftovers from a kill. And they both spend up to 20 hours a day resting or sleeping!

Male lion driving off jackals

How Do Lions Hunt?

Lions often hunt at night. That's when they are most likely to surprise their prey. Lions mostly hunt large animals, such as zebra, buffalo, and wildebeest. Such prey can weigh twice as much as a lion. Prey this big is not easy for one lion to bring down. So when lions hunt, they often work as a team.

Hungry lions begin their hunt by searching for a herd of animals. During most hunts, lions stalk, or creep up on, their prey. Although lions can run fast, many of their prey can run faster. So lions must get as close as they can before they spring at their prey.

When lions work together, they may spread out and circle their prey to cut off escape routes. Then they creep in. Lions use their sharp claws to grab their surprised prey from behind. Or, the lions seize the prey with their powerful jaws. Then they force it to the ground.

Lioness hunting zebra

23

How Do Lions Eat Their Meals?

Lions begin eating soon after they bring their prey to the ground. They use their long canines to tear away large chunks of meat. Since lions have teeth designed for tearing rather than for chewing, they swallow the chunks whole. Lions also use their tongues, which are coarse like sandpaper, to strip away hair and scrape meat off bones.

If there is plenty to eat, a pride eats together. If not, the most powerful, or dominant, males eat first. It might be a while before they finish. A male lion can eat up to 75 pounds (34 kilograms) of meat in just one meal! After the males eat their fill, the lionesses get a turn. The last ones to eat are the cubs, or baby lions.

Lions eat as much as they possibly can at each meal. That's because a week may pass before they catch their next meal. If prey is scarce, lions will eat just about anything they can catch. This includes small mammals, birds, and reptiles.

Lions eating

How Many Cubs Are in a Litter?

A lioness is ready to mate between the ages of 3 and 4. About 3 1/2 months after mating, she gives birth to a litter of one to five cubs.

Lion cubs can't see at birth because their eyes are closed for the first few days of their lives. They are completely dependent on their mother for food and protection. At first, the mother nurses them with her milk. Then, after the cubs are about 6 weeks old, she leads them to an animal she has killed. That's when the cubs get their first taste of meat.

Lions in a pride usually mate around the same time. As a result, the females give birth to their litters around the same time, too. This helps both the mothers and the pride as a whole. A mother lioness can count on other mothers to "cubsit" her young. One female may even nurse another female's cubs.

Lioness with cubs

What Is Life Like for Cubs?

Cubs spend their days sleeping, nursing, and gradually eating more and more meat. They also do a lot of playing. Cubs wrestle and chase each other. They also chase just about anything small that moves. Through playing, cubs learn skills they will need later in life when they must hunt and defend themselves.

In time, a mother lioness weans her cubs, or gradually stops feeding them her milk. From then on, the cubs eat meat. At just over a year, lion cubs are bigger than the adults of most other kinds of wild cats and weigh about 100 pounds (45 kilograms).

Female cubs usually stay with a pride their entire lives. Adult males, however, chase young males from the pride when the younger males turn 2 or 3. Often, the young males wander together until they are about 5. When they are strong enough, they will try to take over a pride and its territory.

Cubs wrestling

29

How Many Kinds of Lions Are There?

Lions that live in Africa are called African lions. Those that live in India are called Asiatic lions. These lions may go by different names, but there is only one species, or kind, of lion.

Thousands of years ago, lions could be found over much of the world. They lived in Africa, Europe, Asia, and even North and South America. Lions probably disappeared from many regions when forests grew too thick, their prey became extinct, and humans overhunted them. Today, the only lions that live outside of Africa are found in one area of India.

Lions that live in Africa and India belong to the same species. But there are differences between them. Lions living in India are smaller than those living in Africa. They also have smaller manes. Because of these slight differences, these two forms of lions are often called by different names.

Asiatic lion

Do Lions Compete with Other Wild Cats?

Lions do compete for prey with other big wild cats, such as leopards and cheetahs. But lions do not compete with the biggest wild cats of all—tigers. The reason that lions and tigers don't compete with each other is that they don't live near each other.

All tigers live in Asia. One form of tiger lives far north in the snow-covered alpine forests of Siberia. But most tigers, like this Bengal tiger, live in warm, tropical habitats. The Bengal tiger is actually the same species as all tigers. But just as an Asiatic lion differs slightly from an African lion, the Bengal tiger differs slightly from other forms of the tiger.

Like most wild cats, except for lions, tigers spend most of their lives on their own. Male and female tigers usually gather to mate between November and April. Three to four months later, a female tiger gives birth to up to six cubs. Usually, though, she gives birth to only two or three cubs.

Bengal tiger

How Big Is a Tiger?

An average adult male tiger weighs about 420 pounds (190 kilograms) and is 9 feet (2.7 meters) long, including its tail. That means that an adult male tiger can be bigger than an adult male lion. But a tiger can grow even bigger than that. The Siberian tiger is the largest wild cat of all. It can weigh nearly 800 pounds (360 kilograms) and measure up to 13 feet (4 meters) long, including its tail!

Siberian tigers are not only bigger than their relatives that live to the south, but their coats are different, too. Siberian tigers grow thick, shaggy coats that help keep them warm during the long, cold winters of the far north. And just like other tigers, Siberian tigers have coats with stripes.

Siberian tiger

Why Are a Tiger's Stripes Important?

A tiger's stripes camouflage *(KAM uh flahzh)* the tiger, or help it blend in with its surroundings. The dark brown or black stripes can cover a tiger from its head to the tip of its long tail. But no two tigers have the same pattern of stripes.

Tigers live in all types of forests, wetlands, and grasslands. Because of their stripes, tigers hunting in these habitats can't be seen by their prey. This helps tigers be very successful predators.

Despite their huge size, tigers are silent and sneaky hunters. Tigers mostly hunt large prey, such as wild pigs and deer. Sometimes, they even hunt young rhinoceroses and elephants. They often hide near rivers and ponds, waiting for prey to come for a drink. Tigers are also excellent swimmers. They sometimes chase prey out into deep waters to make a kill.

Tiger in tall grass

Which Wild Cat Is the Fastest?

The cheetah is the fastest wild cat of all. In fact, a cheetah can run faster than any other land animal. Over short distances, it can sprint up to 70 miles (110 kilometers) an hour!

A cheetah is built for speed. It has a long, slim body and a small head. Its long legs enable it to take huge strides. And its claws are only partially retractable—so they are exposed while the cheetah runs. This gives the animal better traction. And when it makes sharp turns, a cheetah uses its long tail like a rudder to help keep its balance.

A cheetah relies on its great speed to capture fast prey, such as gazelles and antelope. But it can't keep up this speed for more than a few hundred yards. If a cheetah doesn't catch its prey before then, it usually gets tired and the prey gets away.

Cheetah sprinting

39

Where Do Leopards Live?

Leopards have the widest range of all the wild cats that live in Africa and Asia. They live as far west as western Africa and as far east as Korea in Asia. Leopards prowl forests, swamps, deserts, and rocky mountainsides.

Though smaller than lions and tigers, leopards are also large wild cats. They average 7 1/2 feet (2.3 meters) long, including their tails. They weigh up to 160 pounds (73 kilograms). Females are slightly smaller than males.

Leopards are very strong. And they are excellent climbers. After catching their prey, leopards often drag the carcasses, or dead bodies, high up into trees and eat them there. Leopards do this to keep their meals from being taken away by other large animals, such as male lions. Leopards can drag carcasses weighing as much as or more than they do up a tree.

Leopard

Do All Leopards Have Spots?

Yes, all leopards have spots over their bodies. Most leopards are yellowish or tan with black spots. Some leopards, however, are born all black. But even they have spots. A black leopard's fur is so dark that the spots can be hard to see. Take a look at this leopard. Can you see its black spots? Not only do black leopards have spots, but like all leopards, they also have rings on their tails.

A leopard's spots provide excellent camouflage. A leopard often lurks silently among the trees and grass when it hunts. A leopard blends in well with the patterns and shadows of its habitat. This helps it sneak up on prey, such as monkeys, antelope, goats, sheep, and snakes. When prey is near, a hiding leopard rushes out and makes a deadly pounce.

Black leopard

Are All Spotted Wild Cats Leopards?

No, they aren't. For example, a jaguar is not a leopard. But, at first glance, a jaguar and a leopard do look a lot alike. Both wild cats usually have golden or brownish-yellow fur with many black spots. And both are about the same size. So how do you tell these animals apart? Jaguars have stockier builds and wider faces than leopards do. And while leopards are found in Africa and Asia, jaguars live in Mexico, Central America, and South America.

The jaguar is the largest kind of wild cat in the Americas. It can grow up to 8 1/2 feet (2.6 meters) long including its tail and weigh up to 300 pounds (140 kilograms).

Jaguars are excellent climbers. Their short forelegs are strong and help them climb up steep slopes and trees with ease. Jaguars are also superb swimmers. They are good hunters, too. They feed on deer, capybaras, and tapirs.

Jaguar

Which Wild Cat Has Many Names?

What do you call the wild cat in this photo? Some people call it a mountain lion. But this animal has different names, depending on where it lives. These names include cougar, puma, catamount, and panther. Early settlers in the Americas saw these cats climbing on cliffs and mountains. The settlers thought these wild cats looked like female lions. So that's how they got one of their names—mountain lion.

The mountain lion lives throughout North and South America. It can be found in more places than any other wild cat in the Americas. It is also found in many different habitats, including canyons, forests, swamps, deserts, and, of course, mountains. This may be why the mountain lion has so many names.

Mountain lions are skillful predators. They eat just about any animal they can catch. Their prey includes elk, moose, rabbits, and raccoons.

Mountain lion

Which Wild Cats Have "Snowshoes" for Paws?

Lynxes *(LIHNGKS uhz)* are medium-sized wild cats. They live in parts of Europe, Asia, and North America. Many kinds of lynxes live in cold, snowy climates. But cold and snow don't seem to bother them. During winter, these lynxes have thick fur coats. They also have large paws that are covered by thick fur. Their paws act like snowshoes and help them chase their main prey—rabbits and hares— over snow-covered ground.

A lynx has a very distinct look. Its ears are pointed. They are dark brown or black in color. At the end of each ear is a tuft of black hair. A lynx has a short, stubby tail and long fur. At the end of winter, the animal sheds its winter fur. This helps a lynx stay cool when the weather isn't so cold.

Canada lynx

What's So Amazing About a Bobcat?

A bobcat is not much bigger than the average house cat. But a bobcat can kill an animal many times its size. This powerful wild cat hunts animals as big as deer. Usually, though, bobcats prefer smaller prey, such as rabbits, squirrels, mice, and birds.

Bobcats live in parts of North America. Their habitats include forests, deserts, and mountains. Bobcats do most of their searching for food near dawn and dusk each day. In the middle of the day, they hide and rest in tree hollows, small caves, and thick bushes.

Bobcat with prey

What Can a Caracal's Ears Tell You?

A caracal is a golden wild cat that lives in dry regions from Africa to India. A caracal has large black ears. Like a lynx, a caracal has long tufts of hair at the tips of its ears. A caracal's ears look striking. And like the ears of other cat-family members, the caracal's ears also give clues about what the animal is feeling or ready to do.

The caracal you see here is alert. It is watching or listening to something. How can you tell? Its ears are stiff and point straight up. When a caracal is resting, its ears are relaxed, pointing forward and out. If a caracal is frightened, it flattens its ears straight back against its head. When a caracal is ready to attack, it turns its ears toward its back, but it does not completely flatten them.

Caracal

How Did Clouded Leopards Get Their Name?

Despite their name, clouded leopards are not closely related to leopards. Clouded leopards are much smaller than leopards. They weigh between 35 and 55 pounds (16 to 25 kilograms). Clouded leopards do have spots, but their spots are much larger than leopard spots. Many people think their spots look like clouds, so that's how they got their name.

Clouded leopards live in forests in Southeast Asia. They are at home on the ground and in trees. They eat fish, birds, squirrels, monkeys, and wild pigs. Sometimes clouded leopards will even jump down from trees and land on their prey. They kill their prey with their powerful jaws. The jaws of clouded leopards are stronger than the jaws of most other wild cats. Clouded leopards also have the longest canines in relation to their body size.

Clouded leopard

Which Wild Cat Is a Good Fisher?

The fishing cat is a small wild cat that lives near water and is a good fisher. Unlike most pet cats, this wild cat doesn't let a little water bother it. In fact, the fishing cat is an excellent swimmer and diver. But what makes a fishing cat a really good fisher is its patience.

A fishing cat will wait long and quietly near the edge of a stream for fish to swim by. When a fish finally passes, the wild cat lashes out with a paw and bats the fish ashore. Then it quickly bites the fish with its sharp teeth.

Fishing cats live in tropical forests and swamps of southeastern Asia. One of these stocky wild cats weighs up to 33 pounds (15 kilograms).

Fishing cat with fish

Which Wild Cat Is Made of "Spare Parts"?

None are, really. But the serval is a wild cat that looks as if it is made from the leftover parts of other animals. This wild cat has a long, thin body and a small head—like a cheetah. A serval also has long, deerlike legs. To top it off, a serval has long, rounded ears—like those of a wolf.

Servals live in the grasslands and woodlands of Africa. Their prey include mice, hares, rats, and lizards. Even the smallest sounds made by their prey can be picked up by their huge ears. When servals hear prey scuffling around, they use their long legs to leap high up into the air. Then they pounce on their prey. When the servals land, they pin their prey down with their paws.

Serval pouncing

Are Wild Cats in Danger?

Many wild cats are in danger. The Florida panther, a form of the mountain lion, is facing extinction. There are only 30 to 50 of these cats left in the wild. The clouded leopard is also endangered. Scientists believe that this rare wild cat is now extinct in many places where it used to live.

All over the world, wild cats are losing their habitats as people cut down forests and clear grasslands for farms and cities. The cats lose their territories, so they can no longer find food or shelter. And although laws protect many wild cats, many hunters still poach, or hunt these animals illegally.

Today, people are making efforts to protect wild cats. Some governments protect natural lands so these animals will continue to have habitats. Also, some zoos now breed endangered wild cats. Releasing these cats back into their natural habitats may help them flourish in the wild once more.

Clouded leopard

Wild Cats Fun Facts

→ A serval sometimes threatens predators by punching the air with its paws!

→ The caracal is often called the desert lynx because its ears are similar to those of lynxes.

→ A jaguar has a roar that sounds like the bark of a dog.

→ Lions and tigers have mated in some zoos. A liger is a cross between a male lion and a female tiger. A tigon is a cross between a male tiger and a female lion.

→ Scientists think that today's pet cats descended from a small African wild cat that was tamed about 4,000 years ago.

→ A cheetah can sprint from a standstill to its top speed in three seconds.

62

Glossary

brush Shrubs, bushes, and small trees that grow thickly in the woods.

camouflage To blend in with the surroundings.

canine A long, pointed tooth.

carcass The dead body of an animal.

carnivore An animal that eats mostly meat.

cub A baby lion.

dominant The most powerful and leading male lions in a pride.

felidae The scientific name for the cat family.

feline An animal in the cat family, such as a lion, leopard, cheetah, or pet cat.

habitat The area where an animal lives, such as grasslands or desert.

litter A group of baby lions given birth by a mother lioness at one time.

mammal A warm-blooded animal that feeds its young on the mother's milk.

mane The long, heavy hair on the back or around the neck of some animals.

predator An animal that lives by hunting and killing other animals for food.

prey Any animal that is hunted for food by another animal.

pride A group of lions living together.

retractable To be able to draw back or in.

Siberia A large region that extends across northern Asia.

territory An area where an animal lives and which it defends.

tuft A bunch of hairs held together at one end.

wean To gradually get a young mammal used to food other than its mother's milk.

Index

(**Boldface** indicates a photo, map, or illustration.)

For more information about wild cats, try these resources:

Big Cat Conservation, by Peggy Thomas, Twenty-first
   Century Books, 2000.

Big Cats, by John Bonnett Wexo, Wildlife Education.
   1999.

Lynx: Wildcats of North America, by Jalma Barrett,
   Blackbirch Press, 1998.

http://www.nhptv.org/natureworks/bobcat.htm
http://www.oaklandzoo.org/atoz/azlion.html
http://www.pbs.org/kratts/world/eurasia/tiger/
index.html

Wild Cat Classification

Scientists classify animals by placing them into groups. The animal kingdom is a group that contains all the world's animals. Phylum, class, order, and family are smaller groups. Each phylum contains many classes. A class contains orders, an order contains families, and a family contains individual species. Each species also has its own scientific name. Here is how the animals in this book fit in to this system.

Animals with backbones and their relatives (Phylum Chordata)

Mammals (Class Mammalia)

Carnivores (Order Carnivora)

Cats (Family Felidae)

Bobcat	*Felis rufus*
Canada lynx	*Felis canadensis*
Caracal	*Felis caracal*
Cheetah	*Acinonyx jubatus*
Clouded leopard	*Neofelis nebulosa*
Fishing cat	*Felis viverrina*
Jaguar	*Panthera pardus*
Leopard	*Panthera pardus*
Lion (includes African and Asiatic)	*Panthera leo*
Mountain lion (includes the Florida panther)	*Felis concolor*
Serval	*Felis serval*
Tiger (includes Bengal and Siberian)	*Panthera tigris*